Beginner Biography

Wilma Rudolph

Fastest Woman on Earth

by Jeri Cipriano
illustrated by Scott R. Brooks

Red Chair Press   Egremont, Massachusetts

Look! Books are produced and published by Red Chair Press:

Red Chair Press LLC   PO Box 333   South Egremont, MA 01258-0333

www.redchairpress.com

FREE lesson guide at www.redchairpress.com/free-activities

Publisher's Cataloging-In-Publication Data
Names: Cipriano, Jeri S., author. | Brooks, Scott R., 1963- illustrator.

Title: Wilma Rudolph: fastest woman on Earth / by Jeri Cipriano; illustrated by Scott R. Brooks.

Description: Egremont, Massachusetts : Red Chair Press, [2020] | Series: Look! books. Beginner biography | Includes index and resources for further reading. | Interest age level: 005-008. | Summary: "Wilma Rudolph wanted to run and jump like other children. But she had a serious disease that kept her leg from growing well. She did not give up and one day she became a big star winning Olympic gold medals."-- Provided by publisher.

Identifiers: ISBN 9781634409759 (library hardcover) | ISBN 9781634409766 (paperback) | ISBN 9781634409773 (ebook)

Subjects: LCSH: Rudolph, Wilma, 1940---Juvenile literature. | Women runners--United States--Biography--Juvenile literature. | African American women--Biography--Juvenile literature. | African American women track and field athletes--Biography--Juvenile literature. | CYAC: Rudolph, Wilma, 1940- | Women runners--United States--Biography. | African American women--Biography. | African American women track and field athletes--Biography.

Classification: LCC GV1061.15.R83 C56 2020 (print) | LCC GV1061.15.R83 (ebook) | DDC 796.42/092 B--dc23

Library of Congress Control Number: 2019938785

Photo credits: p. 20: © Everett Collection Historical/Alamy; p. 21: © AP Images

Printed in the United States of America

0819 1P CGS20

Table of Contents

Introduction

Wilma Rudolph was born on June 23, 1940, in St. Bethlehem, Tennessee. Wilma weighed less than five pounds at birth. She was the 20th of 22 sisters and brothers.

She was so sick as a child, doctors said she would never walk. But soon she began to run! Wilma ran so fast, she won three gold medals at the Olympics.

"My doctors told me I'd never walk. My mother said I would. I believed my mother."

5

Wilma: The Early Years

Wilma was a sickly baby. When she was 4 years old, she got **polio**. She lost the use of her left leg. Wilma had to wear heavy steel **braces** on her legs. The braces helped her stand and walk.

Good to Know

A new medicine to prevent polio was used starting in 1955. It saved thousands of lives.

Getting Help

Every day, Wilma and her mother traveled 90 miles to and from Nashville. They went to a doctor who used heat and water on her legs. At home, Wilma's mother and **siblings** took turns rubbing her legs.

Pushing Herself

Wilma started hopping on one leg. When she was 11, she began playing basketball in her bare feet. Her father pushed her to **compete** with her sisters and brothers.

Basketball

Wilma wanted to play on her high school basketball team. When the coach picked her older sister, Wilma's father told him he would have to take Wilma as well.

Good to Know

The coach gave Wilma a nickname. He called her *Skeeter* because she was like a mosquito. "You're little, you're fast and you always get in my way."

Becoming a Runner

Wilma played basketball. She also started running on a **track**. She was especially good in short, fast races. As a young teen, she never lost a race.

From College to the Olympics

Wilma began classes at Tennessee State University in September 1957. By 1960, she was ready to run in the **Olympics**.

Wilma won three gold medals for the United States.

Wilma was the first American woman to win three or more medals in one Olympics.

Good to Know

Because the 1960 Olympics were the first to be seen on TV, Wilma was famous when she got home.

Becoming Famous

The governor of her home state wanted to have a parade to honor Wilma. Wilma refused unless all people were allowed to attend—not just white people. Wilma's parade became the first parade in Tennessee open to all people who wanted to be there!

18

President Kennedy invited Wilma to the White House after she won three gold medals.

Timeline: Big Dates in Rudolph's Life

June 23, 1940: Wilma Rudolph is born in Tennessee.

1944: Wilma gets polio and loses the use of her legs.

1949: At age 9, Wilma takes off her leg braces and walks.

1954: Wilma plays basketball in school.

1960: At age 20, Wilma wins three gold medals at the 1960 Olympics in Rome, Italy.

1961: Wilma graduates college and becomes a teacher and a coach.

1963: Wilma marries and has four children.

November 12, 1994: Wilma dies at age 54 from a brain tumor.

Words to Know

brace: an iron device that supports a weak part of the body

compete: try to beat others

Olympics: a sports event that takes place every four years. Athletes come from around the world to play against each other.

polio: a disease that stops children from being able to move their legs

siblings: sisters and brothers

track: a prepared course for runners in a race

Learn More at the Library

(Check out these books to read with others.)

Engfer, Lee. *Wilma Rudolph: Olympic Track Star (Graphic Biographies)*. Capstone, 2006.

Miller, Pat Zietlow. *The Quickest Kid in Clarksville*. Chronicle Books, 2016.

Sherrow, Victoria. *Wilma Rudolph (On My Own Biography)*. Carolrhoda Books, 2016.

Index

About the Author

Jeri Cipriano has written more than a hundred books for young readers. She enjoys reading and finding out new things. She likes to share what she learns.